SPACE TECH

THE INTERNATIONAL SPACE STATION

by ALLAN MOREY

EPIC

BELLWETHER MEDIA • MINNEAPOLIS, MN

EPIC BOOKS are no ordinary books. They burst with intense action, high-speed heroics, and shadows of the unknown. Are you ready for an Epic adventure?

This edition first published in 2018 by Bellwether Media, Inc.

No part of this publication may be reproduced in whole or in part without written permission of the publisher. For information regarding permission, write to Bellwether Media, Inc., Attention: Permissions Department, 5357 Penn Avenue South, Minneapolis, MN 55419.

Library of Congress Cataloging-in-Publication Data

Names: Morey, Allan.
Title: The International Space Station / by Allan Morey.
Description: Minneapolis, MN : Bellwether Media, Inc., 2018. | Series: Epic. Space Tech |
    Audience: Age 7-12. | Includes bibliographical references and index.
Identifiers: LCCN 2016057238 (print) | LCCN 2016058094 (ebook) | ISBN 9781626177017 (hardcover : alk. paper) |
    ISBN 9781681034317 (ebook) | ISBN 9781618912848 (paperback : alk. paper)
Subjects: LCSH: International Space Station–Juvenile literature. | Space stations–Juvenile literature.
Classification: LCC TL797.15 .M67 2018 (print) | LCC TL797.15 (ebook) | DDC 629.44/2–dc23
LC record available at https://lccn.loc.gov/2016057238

Editor: Nathan Sommer   Designer: Steve Porter

Printed in the United States of America, North Mankato, MN.

TABLE OF CONTENTS

THE INTERNATIONAL SPACE STATION AT WORK!

It is November 2, 2000. A **space shuttle** docks at the **International** Space Station (ISS). Its outer **hatch** opens. One American and two Russian **astronauts** float through it. They are the first people to live in this giant space **laboratory**!

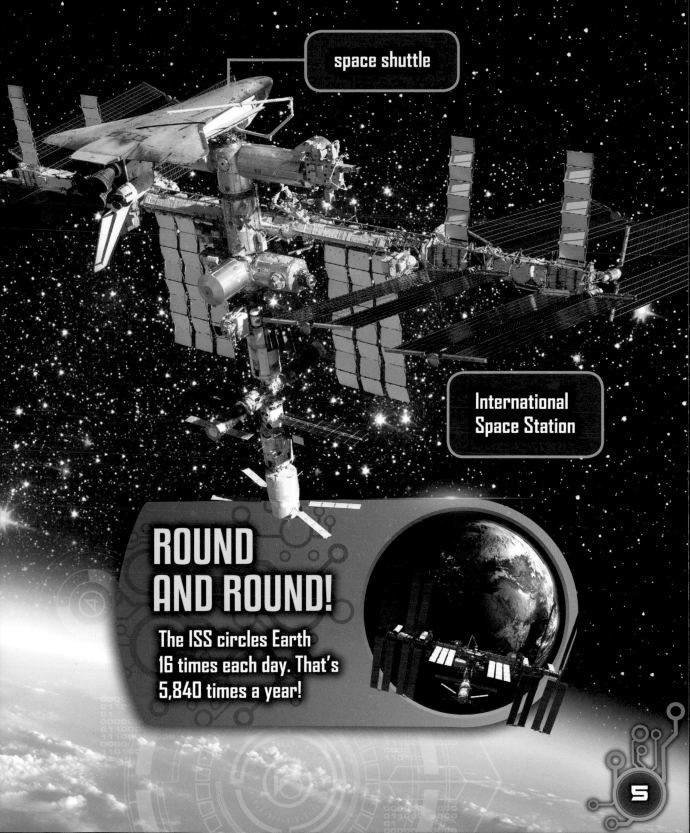

space shuttle

International Space Station

ROUND AND ROUND!

The ISS circles Earth 16 times each day. That's 5,840 times a year!

WHAT IS THE INTERNATIONAL SPACE STATION?

The ISS is the largest machine people have ever put into space. Astronauts live and work aboard it. The ISS **orbits** Earth. It can sometimes be seen in the night sky!

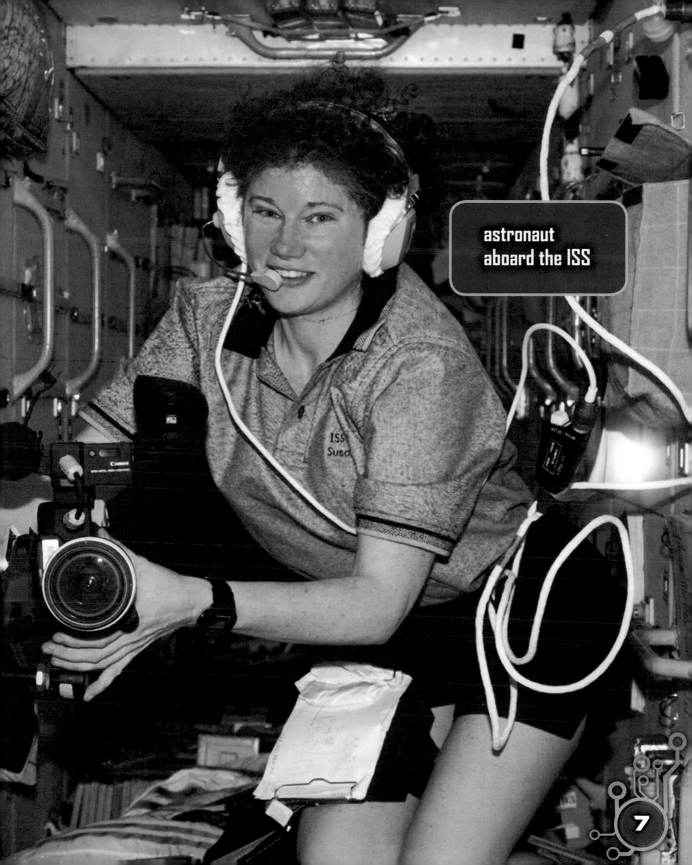

astronaut
aboard the ISS

ISS crew members

Will humans ever live in outer space? If they do, they will need clean air, water, and food. **Crews** on the ISS are learning how to make this possible. They study the effects of living in space.

IT'S A SMALL WORLD!

More than 200 astronauts from 18 countries have visited the ISS.

PARTS OF THE INTERNATIONAL SPACE STATION

It took 13 years to build the International Space Station. Space shuttles carried parts into space. The station's giant robotic arms put the big pieces together. Astronauts went on **spacewalks** to connect the smaller parts. In 2011, the ISS was complete!

space shuttle

Endeavour

the ISS
in 2001

PIECE BY PIECE!

It took more than 115 space flights to build the ISS.

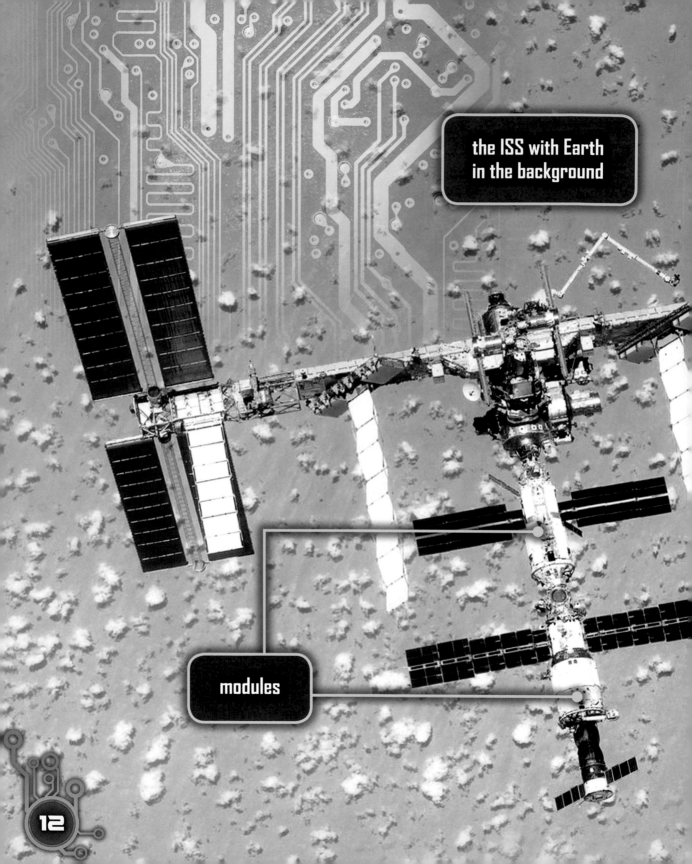

the ISS with Earth
in the background

modules

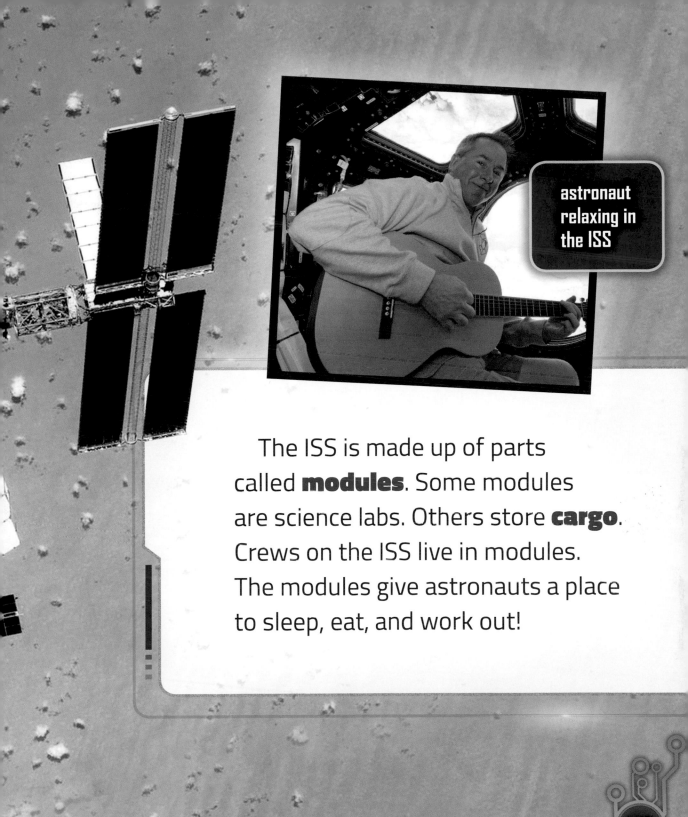

astronaut relaxing in the ISS

The ISS is made up of parts called **modules**. Some modules are science labs. Others store **cargo**. Crews on the ISS live in modules. The modules give astronauts a place to sleep, eat, and work out!

Modules are connected by the **truss**. The truss is the longest part of the ISS. It has **air locks** where **spacecraft** can dock. At its ends are **solar panels**. These power the ISS.

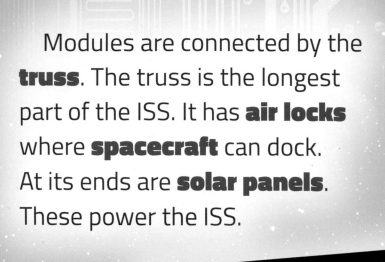

air lock

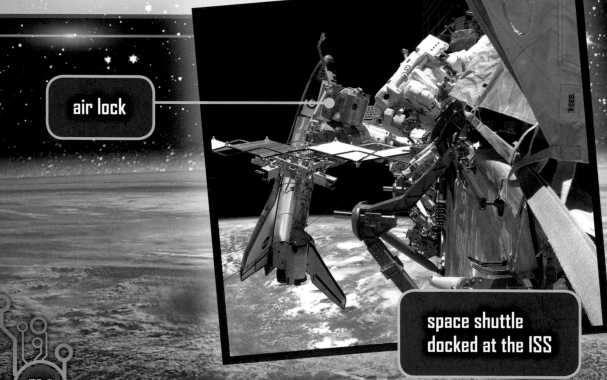

space shuttle docked at the ISS

IDENTIFY THE MACHINE
International Space Station

solar panels

modules

truss

robotic arm

INTERNATIONAL SPACE STATION MISSIONS

The first **mission** to the ISS was in 1998. Many nations sent up pieces to help build the station. Since then, there have been more than 50 missions to the ISS. Astronauts from all over the world use it!

astronaut
working on the ISS

PARTY OF SIX!

Up to six people work on
the ISS at a time.

Astronauts do many experiments aboard the ISS. They want to know how humans can live in space for a long time. They study how to grow food. One day, their work might help humans travel to planets like Mars!

Mars

INTERNATIONAL SPACE STATION SPECS

NAME: INTERNATIONAL SPACE STATION

- location in space: 248 miles (399 kilometers) above Earth

- speed: 17,500 miles (28,164 kilometers) per hour

- length (truss): 357.5 feet (109 meters)

- height: 66 feet (20 meters)

- width (solar panel wingspan): 240 feet (73 meters)

- mission: to serve as an international laboratory in space where astronauts can live and work

- first time in space: 1998

GLOSSARY

air locks—compartments used to allow astronauts to travel safely between a space station and a spacecraft

astronauts—people trained to travel and work in outer space

cargo—goods carried by a spacecraft

crews—people who work together on the ISS

hatch—a door in a vehicle

international—related to two or more countries

laboratory—a place where scientists perform experiments

mission—a task or job

modules—parts of a larger structure

orbits—circles around an object

solar panels—devices that collect sunlight and turn it into energy

space shuttle—a reusable spacecraft that carries people and cargo between Earth and outer space

spacecraft—any vehicle used to travel in outer space

spacewalks—trips outside of a spacecraft

truss—a long metal support structure

TO LEARN MORE

AT THE LIBRARY

Nelson, Maria. *Life on the International Space Station*. New York, N.Y.: Gareth Stevens Publishing, 2013.

VanVoorst, Jenny Fretland. *Space Stations*. Minneapolis, Minn.: Pogo, 2017.

Waxman, Laura Hamilton. *Exploring the International Space Station*. Minneapolis, Minn.: Lerner Publications, 2012.

ON THE WEB

Learning more about the International Space Station is as easy as 1, 2, 3.

1. Go to www.factsurfer.com.

2. Enter "International Space Station" into the search box.

3. Click the "Surf" button and you will see a list of related web sites.

With factsurfer.com, finding more information is just a click away.

INDEX

The images in this book are reproduced through the courtesy of: Alan Uster, front cover (Earth/moon); NASA, front cover (ISS), pp. 5 (ISS-SpecFeature), 6-13 (all), 14 (framed ISS/space shuttle), 15 (ISS), 16-17 (all), 18-19 (astronaut), 20-21; Aphelleon, pp. 2-3; Andrey Armyagov, pp. 4-5 (Earth); Stocktrek Images, Inc./ Alamy, pp. 4-5 (ISS); MarcelClemens, p. 5 (Earth-SpecFeature); Juergen Faelchle, pp. 14-15 (Earth); 3Dsculptor, pp. 19 (Mars satellite), 21 (ISS).